A GREYT CHRISTMA

by Miriam Payne

Illustrated by Anne-Marie Sonneveld

Published by Filament Publishing Ltd
16 Croydon Road
Beddington, Croydon, Surrey,
CR0 4PA, United Kingdom.
www.filamentpublising.com
Telephone: +44(0)208 688 2598

A Greyt Christmas Tail by Miriam Payne

Illustrated by Anne-Marie Sonneveld
www.ams-illustrations.com

© 2017 Miriam Payne

ISBN 978-1-912256-22-8

Printed by Print2Demand Ltd.

The presents were opened and would you believe -
Reindeer hats for both dogs from under the tree.
And Ramsey he chuckled and curled up with Blue
"Silly hoomans, dear Blue girl - if only they knew!"

Then Santa he climbed back up onto his sleigh
"God bless you sweet dogs. Ho! Ho! Ho!" and away.
Before they knew it the hoomans came in
"Merry Christmas stinkies" they both did sing.

For Christmas please comfort all those dogs too
With a warm bed, a toy and a big bowl of food.
Please bring them some love and a nice meaty bone
But most of all, Santa, a forever home".

"Oh Santa we's lucky dogs, this much we know
With our bed and our hoomans who love us both so.
There's others just like us who don't have a home,
They're lonely and scared or in kennels alone.

"Dear houndies without you, what would I have done?
Christmas would've been ruined if you hadn't run.
Now sleep, for your humans will soon be awake
But first, I must ask you - what wish do you make?"

"Just a couple more presents to go and we're through
How lucky we were to find Ramsey and Blue!"
And then they were home, the dogs fell into bed
Exhausted. "Thank you, thank you!" he said.

Faster and faster and faster they ran
Delivering presents all over the land.
"Oh Rudolph", said Santa, "I think we just might
Visit ALL the good children and get home tonight!

With a pull and a jingle, before they both knew
The two faithful friends ran so fast that they flew!
O'er the houses they soared, up, up, up so high
Their little legs running, their hearts filled with pride.

"Oh Ramsey", cried Blue, "I don't know if I can".
"Don't worry", said Ramsey, "Just hold my hand".
Then Santa yelled "Rudolph, show them what to do -
On Dancer! On Comet! On Ramsey! On Blue!"

"Well ok", said Santa, "We'll give it a try"
And he harnessed them up to the reindeer nearby.
"C'mon little houndies you'll have to be brave
The night's almost over, we've Christmas to save".

"Blue's so fast Santa, she used to compete
And I'm strong, I can pull; let us try and you'll see.
We won't let you down Santa, this much I swear
We's elvses you see and we'll run through the air".

"It's cold at the North Pole, I knew they were ill
We had no choice, it's Christmas - there's stockings to fill"
"We'll help!" said Ramsey. "We'll pull your sleigh.
We can run, it's adventure. What do you say?

With a crash and a clatter. They woke with a start.
The great big red sleigh had crashed right in their yard!
"Oh Santa what happened?" Ramsey cried.
"My reindeer are poorly", the jolly man sighed.

Christmas Eve; two dogs tucked up warm in their beds
Dreams of sausage and rabbits were filling their heads.
With their Christmas coats on, so cosy were they
When, from over the fence there came a sleigh

MIRIAM PAYNE

After 15 years as a journalist both in the UK and USA during which I was lucky enough to win an Emmy Award with NBC News, I left to spread my wings in PR. Writing has always been a passion but I'm an accidental author; the ideas and stories are formed while walking Ramsey and Blue in order to stop them from pulling. You might see me walking around Wigan talking to the dogs and who knows - that chat might become my next manuscript!

RAMSEY AND BLUE

RAMSEY is a 5-year-old lurcher who was abandoned as a puppy. He was found by Foal Farm Animal Rescue in Biggin Hill and bounced into our lives aged 7 months.

BLUE is a 7-year-old ex-racing greyhound who came to us via her owner/trainer when she retired at the age of 4.

You make us laugh, you make us cry (Ramsey), we can't imagine our lives without you x

Acknowledgements

Dave – You and me, we're invincible together.
You see me at my worst and you love me anyway…thank you x

Mum and Dad – for always believing in me and daring to dream,
thank you for all your love and support x

Sarah Kingdon, Marie Higgins and Emma Maher – we can't thank you
enough for choosing us to love Ramsey and Blue

Anne-Marie Sonneveld – never in our wildest dreams did we imagine
how perfectly you would capture their personalities!

Bargecrafts – for your beautiful coats which inspired this story

WHAT PEOPLE ARE SAYING

"I love this story. And I LOVE dogs! I would like to visit Ramsey & Blue one day and give them a big hug. Their wish was a beautiful thing."

Hallie-Jae, age 10

" Ramsey & Blue are so kind. I wish I can be like them one day.
I also wish I can have a pink house like that one with a dog of my own."

Sienna-Rae, age 4

"Those stinkies are heroes! They are strong. They can fly.
And they saved Christmas."

Alfie-Jude, age 3

"This special story has touched the hearts of our entire family from beginning to end! This fairy tail truth spreads a message of love and happiness with a twist of fun and adventure. Everything that life should be. Ramsey and Blue...we love you! X"

Kate (mum)